LIGHT AND MATTER:
Photographs and Poems of Iowa

PAUL BROOKE

Campbell & Lewis Publishers
West Des Moines, Iowa

Copyright © 2008 by Paul Brooke. All rights reserved. No part of this book may be reproduced, scanned, or distributed in any printed or electronic format without permission. All photographs copyright © 2008 by Paul Brooke. No photographs may be reproduced, scanned, or distributed in any printed or electronic format without permission.

First Edition. Published and printed in the United States of America by Campbell & Lewis Publishers, an imprint of Wheaton Partners, Inc., 280 South 79th Street, Suite 1401, West Des Moines, Iowa 50266.

Printed by Signature Book Printing, www.sbpbooks.com

Book orders: 1-866-405-1300   www.ForBetterBooks.com

13 Digit ISBN 978-0-9771489-6-7
10 Digit ISBN 0-9771489-6-3

Book design by Katie Fox, Fox Marketing and Design, College Station, Texas. www.foxmarketingdesign.com

Dedicated to Corly and Dawn

Table of Contents

Thunderclouds	1
Introduction	4
Intoxication	6
Hawthorn Berries	7
Fur of the Mole	8
Mole in Hand	9
Krummholz	10
Stunted Tree	11
Metabolism	12
Hummingbird in Bush	13
Cedar Ramage	14
Wild Turkey	15
Gallagh-Gunley	16
Harvest Moon	17
Filchers	18
Abandoned Farm House	19
Monet's Water Gardeners	20
Yellow Waterlily	21
Falconry	22
Harris Hawk on Glove	23
Writing Spider	24
Orb Weaver	25
Sound Animals	26
Curled Woolly Bear Caterpiller	27
Light and Matter	28
Overlit Houses	29
Ephemerals	30
White Trout Lily	31
The Morals of Morel Hunting	32
Morel Mushroom	33
The Farm Pond	34
Illuminated Corn	35
Fawn After a Rain	35
Redolence	36
Raspberry	37
Delivery	38
Cardinal in Winter	39

Rara Avis	40
Owl at Dusk	41
Kingfisher	42
Kingfisher #1	43
Miter	44
Bishop's Cap	45
Bloodroot	46
Bloodroot Flower	47
Mining Bees	48
Bee in Lady Slipper	49
Anomalies	50
White Bluebell	51
Ritual Undoing	52
Monarch on Coneflower	53
Eagle over the Skunk River	54
Eagle over the Rift	55
Lovers at Night	56
Pasqueflower	57
Art Gallery	58
Woman in Garden	59
Runway	60
Damselfly on Hosta	61
Fourth of July Fireworks	62
Explosive Pasqueflower	63
The Interconnectedness of Things	64
Purple Waterlily	65
Red Fox Pup	65
Bee in Anemone	65
A Few Secrets	66
Wild Grasses in Sunlight	67
Emersion	68
Fire	69
Murmur	70
Steaming River	71
Afterword	72
Bee on Coneflower	73

Introduction

Past

After traveling the world from Mexico to Mongolia, I realize that Iowa grounds me. It's the rhythm of living here, the night harvests of corn, the quick lives of wildflowers, the wing marks of a barred owl in the snow. Iowa makes me slow down and internalize the land. Not get distracted.

I grew up in rural Iowa in Treynor and Minden. In those years, I began to explore the hillsides, finding stray turkey and hawk feathers. I knew there was more to the land than just corn and beans: there were clues to uncover about animal behavior, migrations. I read books on wildlife and began memorizing the genus species. Hours were spent walking gravel roads spying kestrels or the loner fox out on the prowl.

It wasn't long before I was thinking about college and selected Iowa State University for Fisheries and Wildlife Biology. My plan was simply to become a wildlife biologist and study large mammals in the arctic. Before graduation, I worked in the northern part of Alaska near Nuiqset, a native village, where I completed survey work on migratory birds.

During my time in Alaska, I spent whole days on my own, collecting and drying plants, taking photographs of arctic fox and enormous herds of caribou, writing small but intense poems, and hoping to spy the rare gyr-falcon. I only had twenty rolls of film for three months and I made that film last. Some of the photographs I shot were transformative and I began to love the stalking and capturing of images.

One late night as I rested in my tent contemplating my next move, I came to realize that my home place was Iowa, and I missed its rhythms. I also realized that I wanted to be a poet and a teacher. I returned to Iowa to finish my degree and then to pursue my Masters, then my Ph.D. in English.

Poetry became a mechanism to comment on environmental issues and loss. Nowhere is the impact on the environment greater than in the state of Iowa. We have lost ninety percent of our wetlands. Our prairie remnants barely survive, only occupying less then one-tenth of one percent of our land. Iowa has begun the process of making land wild again. Citizens are planting prairies with wild seed, allowing our ditches to grow thick with native flowers, and seeing the value of protecting our few parcels of oak-hickory forests.

Within *Light and Matter*, a shift occurs. The narrator throws off his life of form and urban living for an underground existence. We track him as he notices the nuances of place, the deep connection with plants, animals, and landscape. He literally becomes an underground man. But unlike Dostoevsky's underground man, he actually becomes a better man. He internalizes the wildness around him and allows it to guide and shape who he is. In the end, he returns to the city, fulfilled and centered, ready to love.

Present
As a poet, I envision the world through images. Images grab me and set new poems in motion. This collection is a culmination of work, starting with light and moving into matter. The eye picks up light, tucks an image away and later turns it into deeper matter. Enough matter will generate a strong poem. A lack of matter makes the poem seem lackluster.

The same holds true for photography. It takes the right light, lens, shutter speed, composition, place and time to make the image sing. My theory is that it takes one thousand clicks of the shutter to make one truly outstanding image. Over the past year, I calculate I have shot over fifteen thousand images. Many of the images presented in *Light and Matter* are one in one thousand, literally.

For this collection, I concentrated on images that complimented the poems themselves. Mostly I worked forward, writing the poem first and then taking the right photograph. I've laid on the ground mere meters from foxes, traveled far to photograph wild turkeys, and searched frantically for woolly bear caterpillars. Towards the end of the project however, I actually reversed the process. I shot the photographs and worked backwards. In the case of the kingfisher, the orb weaver, the morel, the bishop's cap, the mining bees, the bluebells and the monarch, all of these poems sprang organically from the image.

This collection seeks to record the natural beauty of Iowa and its richness through light and matter, through photography and poetry. I hope it is clear how much I care for this state and its wild places.

Paul Brooke

Intoxication

—a lyric for my father-in-law—

In the late autumnal heat,
the hawthorn berries over ripen,
polished like purple-red glass,
fermenting in their delicate casks.

The gutters are full of oak leaves
in the late autumnal heat.
The prairie has gone unburned,
the garden weedy and unturned.

So I am left in this house,
windows painted shut, not a relief
of breeze, dust coating the slick
cases full of shells and knick-

knacks. Your gardening tools
sit out back in the greenhouse,
reddening with oxide, slowly
locking themselves onto the floor

in the late autumnal heat.
The waxwings devour clusterfuls
of the intoxicating berries;
they sway drunk and play heavily

upon the branches of the hawthorn
in the late autumnal heat,
I laugh until my sides hurt:
your vacant chair no comfort.

Fur of the Mole

While I was transplanting wild columbine,
a mole poked his nose out of his burrow.
Lately my writing hasn't been going well.
There are constant intrusions, interruptions.

A mole poked his nose out of his burrow;
I had a choice: my hands or the pitchfork.
There are constant intrusions, interruptions.
My mind isn't right; I doubt my words,

I had a choice: my hands or the pitchfork;
I chose my hands and uprooted him.
My mind isn't right; I doubt my words,
I don't believe anyone will ever read my work.

I chose my hands and uprooted him;
I never knew how strangely beautiful a mole was.
I don't believe anyone will ever read my work.
The mail keeps bringing generic rejections.

I never knew how strangely beautiful a mole was,
with his sleek chromed fur and paddled claws.
The mail keeps bringing generic rejections.
Writer-friends have new books and readings.

With his sleek chromed fur and paddled claws,
the mole deserves to master the underground.
Writer-friends have new books and readings,
while I find countless ways of distracting myself.

Krummholz

*—Krummholz is a German word meaning
"crooked wood." Krummholz trees are abraded
and take on a dwarfed and gnarled look—*

Pummeled by arctic wind and ice crystals,
the black spruce was stunted and twisted.
Several more years and I'll go up for tenure
if I teach well and publish a hundred poems.

The black spruce was stunted and twisted,
bare on one side, burdened on the other.
If I teach well and publish a hundred poems,
I'll secure my position. If not, I'll be fired.

Bare on one side, burdened on the other,
the tree lived by taking the shape of the land.
I'll secure my position. If not, I'll be fired;
I won't be able to find academic work.

The tree lived by taking the shape of the land,
and now a community exists under its shade.
I won't be able to find academic work,
so each day I bend, writing at my desk,

And now a community exists under its shade,
and each night the stars seem farther away.
So each day I bend, writing at my desk.
my body contorting against the stress.

Metabolism

—for those who suffer from bulimia—

a hummingbird is trapped in my garage;
I scare her out after an hour. she veers
a short distance and perches on the verge
of the driveway. going inside, I dislodge

a spoon from the kitchen drawer and fill
with purchased nectar. I transfer
the influorescence, strange metallic flower,
out to the hummingbird, the little

thin tongue straws up the mixture;
the more she drinks the more she brightens,
the wings slowly start to fan, then blur,
amazing natural machines;

the ruby-throat is liberated; one push
catapults her to the wild of the lilac bush.

Cedar Ramage

The turkey shifts amidst the cedar ramage,
stretches, unlocks his grip, and listens.
The hunter purrs and yelps. Wearing camouflage,

he blends with shoot and flower montage.
Scratching in the leaves, the man imitates hens.
The turkey shifts amidst the cedar ramage.

Earlier, the hunter created an entourage,
a flock of inflated decoys spun by wind.
The hunter purrs and yelps wearing camouflage.

A fox emerges, recognizing the stiff mirage
of birds. She leaves her den unattended.
The turkey shifts amidst the cedar ramage,

But nothing can deter him, the hens barrage
him with calls. His plumage is copper glisten.
A hunter purrs and yelps wearing camouflage.

This turkey knows of shotgun damage,
Having been hunted now by many men.
The turkey shifts amidst the cedar ramage.
The hunter purrs and yelps wearing camouflage.

Gallagh-Gunley

—a Droighneach, an Irish form—

The farmhands gather to eat and all seem delighted;
harvest of the dried corn is done in the bottomland,
and I'm struck by a guth or a puth of tobacco.
Both seem to hold memories of Ireland.

I've forgotten most of the language, most everything,
but there sings from this ground a rún, a harvest moon,
gallagh-gunley, spreading its shape across stubble fields,
across streams, and across the sea. The harvest moon

once brightened the heather fields of my ancestors,
moonlight poured on their backs as they sheepherded
near craggy bluffs. That same moon is out, shimmering
on us; the men finish supper, and they realize

they must gather the rest of the crop, combining
before gushing rains muddy the fields, rendering
them impassable. I reap all night, imagining
mounds of grain, dreaming of my farming ancestry.

Filchers

*—a casbairdne, an Irish form, without
trisyllabics at the end of each line—*

Cursed badgers burrow under
the upheaved floors. Hairs mess
the boards and stairs. Creatures stir
when we enter the fetid farmhouse;

we have stopped to filch beams and
lost antiquities. We scope
out cupola, attic, and
walls with axe and hammer, hope-

ful with each swing we might find
a fine old hoard, some buried
coin, but nothing is left behind.
This house—I now believe—lies

keeled over, a sunken ship,
a bit dry, blowing to powder
among prairie grass, slipping
and losing to pull's power,

We unhinge the handmade doors,
undock brass fixtures, unload
mast-sized beams out of the floors,
uncover strips of old oak,

leaving the great shape to smolder
forty more years, still witness
to the old wreck, reminder
of farms, foreclosed and cursed.

Monet's Water Gardeners

—a rannaicheacht ghairid, an Irish form—

his lilies
wait inside to miss the freeze
in black bags in the basement,
clipped and bent, anxious to squeeze

up tendrils
of stalks and dozens of thrills
for the water gardener
whose age has whittled his skill.

he'd go wading,
preening each plant: removing
brown growth, deadheading spent blooms,
dusting luminous, stunning

even him-
self with the results. those whims
had to end. the gardener
remembers Monet, the brim

of his wide
hat nodding on the bankside,
as he prepared his brushes
and his crushed paints. the boat slides

by, Monet's
pond workers stop for the day;
the boat is crammed with offal,
beautiful lily rafts sway.

the water
gardener sadly ponders
the scene. the leaves are decayed
and yellowed. the flowers are

brown corpses,
floating face down. His senses
cannot ignore the eyesores,
the deformed look of lilies.

Falconry

—a séadna, an Irish form—

Flying berkuts, Mongols hunted
hundred-pound wolves. Kubla Khan
kept hundreds of falcons.   Britain's
hawks sinned, herons mostly slain.

Falconers now seek a balance
between hunger and the need
to overpower, no longer
misreading nature. I feed

my young; I do not slay simply
to slay. I begin with a cling
to the aerie, where the tiny
fledgling can be found, its wings

not ready. Hours of training—
teaching the young the hand—
are spent every day; wisely,
I find only fresh game and

choice meats. When full grown, the rufter's
rehood and the jesses tied.
The lure is then twirled and lengthened;
I slide off hood, let her glide

flat, then she rises; she's scanning
sky. She feels a thousand eyes
sweeping over her; there's terror
inside her turn of wings. I

read the writing, these blue pages
of pursuit, scripture etched by
talons; this raptured crowd allured
by style, culture, and reigned flight.

Writing Spider

*"in this deliberate burying
of yourself underground for
forty years out of sheer pain."*
— Notes from Underground

I decode this pattern
among prairie grasses:
inverted EKG, razor blade
scrapings of cocaine, zipper
of mildew, sleep of ancient
ones, a miniature billboard,
or bumpersticker. Somehow
each morning, the web
tumbles with bodies, dumb
luck moths or burned out
fireflies. Is it product
placement? The candy
bar or **People** magazine
near the checkout counter?

Hordes charge through,
eventually succumbing
to urges, splurging
on unnecessaries,
hopeful for better skin
or longer sex. I once
fell, suckered by such ploys,
but no more. I burn
my clothes, wriggle bare-
naked through tunnels,
traced upon limestone scarps,
to my lair, to touch dried
berries and salted meats,
blankets and tarps. I will
write like the spider,
lightness from the belly,
darkness from within.

Sound Animals

Cars hum the pavement,
their headlights identifying

mammals only by eye shine:
set too close, green or yellow,

small white strobes. The animal,
terrified by noise, does

not pass on the hard place
scraped by sound animals,

does not approach
their wooden nests or

mechanical legs. Undone
by noise, the animal keeps

away from their barking
skulks and rotating

greeneaters; it lives
happily off the droppings

of trees and the soft insides
of fruit. In the solace

of night, when the sound
animals are idle, it listens

for the smallest
murmurings: an aphid's

wingbeat, a woolly bear's
bristling, the muffled flap

of an owl stretching over
the heaviness of the earth

and then the animal
dreams in pitched silence,

scenes brushing over:
like eyelashes of wild deer,

like wingbeats of hawkmoths,
scenes brushing over:

mild, sumptuous, humanless.

Light and Matter

A couple builds a glass house
near a river; it is lit like a small city
driven by unlimited wattage.

Their lives are all
frenetic energy, electrons
bouncing in constricted space.

No children, two black Saabs,
no pets, fourteen-hour-a-day jobs,
frozen dinners consumed

at different times, television,
bed. Never sex, only arguments.
Each fight ignites the eventual implosion.

Each night, they sink into themselves
like collapsing stars, saying
not a word, slipping

into silence,
into absolute nothingness.

Ephemerals

oh how I wait for them
beneath the snowmelt

bright cousins appearing
unexpectedly at a reunion
driving up the gritty roads
in sleek green cars
cans of beer hidden
between their legs
the bitter nectar
helping them to blaze
incandescent
in their short-bursted lives

The Morals of Morel Hunting

To hunt morels, I rise early,
faithful, a little mesh sack
tied to my waist. Hours pass.

By every sagging elm, nothing.
By every rotted log, nothing.
Broken stems and trampings.

Reason is now overwhelming
my faith. I am sinking
into a morel abyss, a quagmire

of sporeless emptiness.
On the rocky coast, a beacon
flashes ahead, a single morel,

scrumptious fruit, light and airy.
I carry it home in my hand
like a sacred artifact.

That afternoon, my neighbor
waves me over: "Look what
I found, hundreds of morels.

Bagfuls. Like to buy some?"
"No thanks. I have enough."
Dumbstruck, I stagger home

to my kitchen, where a single
morel waits in a small bowl.
Dipped in egg yolk, rolled

in bread crumbs, the morel
fries to a crispy brown, meager,
but enough to fulfill me.

The Farm Pond

That summer I came
to learn wild plants
and tracking timber.
There was peace
in the sun
diminishing after
a hot day. Deer
stood knee-high
in the water and knew
the sanctuary
of thickets and tall corn.
Circling the pond
were the fluorescent
burn of fireflies,
a thousand flickers
of energy, and
the swoop
of the nighthawk,
scooping mouthfuls
of mayflies.

The pond held
a kaleidoscope
of colors and shapes:
great blue herons,
wild grapes, swarms
of mosquitoes, scaly-
tailed muskrats,
lacewings, damselflies.

The pond held
wild berries:
tender and full.
The tingle
of their dark blood
stained my teeth
and tongue.
Their taste lingered.

Their seeds,
fragments of marrow,
pass through me
as if I were a waxwing,
a bird, wavering
on a slender branch.

The pond busied me
with willow whistles,
largemouth bass,
and jumping frogs.
The pond kept
me from the dark
I had seen others in,
thick and murky
as the boot-sucking mud.

That summer
a friend of mine
was killed. His body
crushed. I came
to know wild plants
and tracking
through timber.
Bent leaf.
Trace of hoof.
Musk. Scrapings.
The bed of grass
still warm
from the fleeing deer.

Redolence

Foraging nocturnally,
lilies are luminaries; raspberries
are ancient pheromones.

Interlaced with thorns,
the black locust pricks my ear;
I navigate the trail set

by sharp little moons of white-tailed
deer. I can smell her earthy, blackish,
musky odor, out brambling

in the raspberries, smell her in the curled
edges of leaves, in photographs blackened
by the sun. She has lain down

too long under the wings
of crows, too long under the blacker
shadows of bur oaks. Even if all

my senses leave me save one, she will
be the fragrances in my forest, my purest
recognitions: sweet, herbal, perfumed.

Delivery

—for my wife

Father, I grieved each day.
One apple sat on the counter.
Blood smeared the wall.

You protected those days
I didn't know or recognize.
I turned around and there you were

shaking the snow from your coat.
The airport buzzed with missed
connections, bright packages.

You held me as I cried,
relieved in delivering my wrecking news
the day before Christmas.

Mother doesn't condemn you.
Certainly I don't. I love you,
my little macushla berry.

Tonight, I stand at the back door,
my new husband washing the dishes,
and missing your presence,

something unexpected happens:
on the hawthorn, a cardinal
shakes the snow from his feathers.

Rara Avis

Squawking and beak clicking,
a young barred owl clings
to the base of an oak trunk.

Its perception of flight
is not yet formed; its body feathers
are all down and barely grown.

The adults caterwaul and screech,
calling out: my child has fallen
down a well. They know innately

there is no chance for recovery,
no miraculous climb to the nest cavity,
no divine reversal of gravity;

I ponder the selection, my
own intervention in this scheme:
passer-by or saviour? predator or

pray? man or god? I leave,
gather what I need, and return.
In the place of the owlet,

I drop an offering of carrion.
Taking the owlet in my hand,
it is surprisingly light in weight.

I climb the tree, delivering it
into the opening. I am now
somewhere between earth

and heaven. I am now closer,
I am now nearer to selflessness.
Waiting above me in the heavy

branches, the owls are silhouettes
against the brackish sky;
they are dark, enigmatic angels.

Kingfisher

A scold. A flash of blue.
Minnows scatter like criminals

into alleyways of cattails.
One does not escape, rings widen,

windshield shattering on impact.
Victim carried off on a stretcher.

Within the blind, I am a bystander.
Breathless, whispering my God,

my God. The kingfisher is illumination.
a constellation of water droplets,

sheen of metal blue, crested.
Police-sharp in dress,

eye mirrored and alert.
A bonfire, couches burning.

Chased through yards and gardens.
The police officer huffing and puffing,

falling behind in the darkness.
I ran and ran, groping for a hide.

Behind a woodpile I laid
one hour, mistaken identity.

The creature squirms
trying to slide itself loose.

Thwack. Thwack. Eyes closed,
the kingfisher smacks the fish

against the stick. Immobile.
Delirious. I am the only

witness to this carnage.

Miter

Not quite snowflakes,
five-pointed, blurred.
Not quite blown glass
or folded paper.

Lilliputian-sized, you
are a gathering of bishops
under cathedrals of oaks.
I kneel at your feet,

not quite praying,
paralyzed by guilt.
Delicate, you lean under
the weight of dew.

In the wind, you touch
my shoulder with grace,
forgiving my absence
this fine Sunday morning.

Bloodroot

I never knew the earth
could bleed until I met you.
Digging in the moist soil,
uncarefully, I cut the root,
salmon-colored, sap ooze.

My failings brought us
rotting vegetation
and delineation, words
forming. I keep asking,
"Are you okay? Are you?"

We go on. Years tangle.
The woodcock returns.
Hunters forget. Bloodroot
flowers unroll like gauze,
their veins fuse the wounds.

Mining Bees

Drilling a bolt hole,
a gas pocket erupts,
corrupting stability.
The mine collapses,
rock and hot metal.

Beating a hammer
against torn girders,
the survivors breathe
shallow prayers
in the methane deep.

"Please forgive me,
and help me avoid
sinning again."

One mining bee
enters the opening.
No exit, it flounders
beating itself
against the walls.

Covered in yellow soot,
the bee climbs out.
A new set of workers
wait, lunch buckets
in hand, trembling.

Anomalies

*"There is no greater anomaly in nature
than the bird that cannot fly."*
  —Darwin's The Origin of Species

Than the cell that does not divide,

Than the artery that sends blood in reverse,

Than the nighthawk that is sleepless all day,

Than the white bluebell that never darkens,

Than the amputated leg that feels phantom pain,

Than the novelist who does not want fame,

Than the stag that never sheds its antlers,

Than the couple who does not bicker,

Than the meteor that is gelatinous,

Than the tornado that is luminous,

Than the moon that strays from its orbit.

Ritual Undoing

I unfold myself
in the morning air,

wings like crimped paper,
ornate, brush-stroked.

Knees ache, elbow pops,
the body unhinges,

grappling with demise.
Forget hemorrhage,

forget tourniquet.
I never speak of it.

The girl leaving the room.
The boy receiving undo

attention from the priest.
The woman covering

her bruise with make up.
The man sleeping

with his clothes on.
I didn't speak of it.

Why do we turn?
Who taught us

to look away.
Now I don't.

Eagles Over the Rift

It cracks once a day,
an assault of branches.
Parents shriek and wheel
at trespassers. The young
flatten, fuzz white,
nest litter, a rabbit's leg,
backbones of redhorses.
Granted, everything
accumulates, possessions,
truckloads of furniture
made of sticks and twigs,
a heft certain to split.
Somehow the eagles
know. The chicks
fledge. Troutlilies
unfurl their green tongues.
The nest collapses.
Tree cleaved in two.
The young too grown
to alter their flight.

Lovers at Night

I pencil-sketch
influorescent
wildflowers
as they butter
the forest floor
with more grains
of iridescent pollen.

Two lovers, naked,
are caught in the dark,
the dark is strobed
by fireflies, the lovers'
skin is beautiful
as tin, their breath
is smoke in the chill.

Two lovers, naked,
are caught in art,
in the art of touch,
of honey, of nectar,
of drops of pollen,
all resins of nature.

I observe concealed
in the underbrush,
blending perfectly,
my hair and skin,
moss green and brown.

I have drawn touch
for solitude, love
for glimpsing.
And in the edges
and patterns
of this forest,
as the lovers dress
and unbramble
their hair, their
passion makes me whole.

Art Gallery

The canvas evolves.
I awaken and stumble out
to view the tranquility,
the luster of leaves,
almost silken in their morning holds.

Last night, you whispered,
We won't last another year,
We never even leave this house.

Now you're out in your garden
in the early spring,
imagining potential blooms—
the bottoms of your pantlegs wet,
your hands placed on your hips—
imagining how the irises purple,
the buttercups yellow,
the astilbes redden.

I'd call out to you and you'd
look up—like a stalky bloom—
and wave, slow and easy.

The beauty of the garden
comes forth from shaping
in the hands of its gardeners;
we've fretted over our marriage,
never imagining its potential bloom.

Runway

On a penisula of shale,
damselflies hover
in the swales, gyrating
hither and thither;
finite passages made
on coal-black wings
and metallic fuselages.

Fourth of July Fireworks

Imagine the sky
above the forest
blackened:
darkest carbon
painting a starless night.
Imagine lying
on a grassy blanket
silently, only whispers
pressing between us.
Imagine, the night
made equally
from our bodies
touching
and the ebony air.
And sleep,
coming over us
in heated waves
as we drift away
holding hands
to share
the same vivid dream
with birds
singing lullabies
in a sky of dirt.
Imagine, waking
in a ruckus
of floral explosions:
shooting star,
blue aster,
firewheel,
purple iris,
tiger lily,
snapdragon,
sunflower,
wild rose,
morning glory.

The Interconnectedness of Things

        barking treefrog
       smoketree
prairie smoke
prairie false indigo
         indigobush
             bush clover
              owl clover
         spotted owl
     red-spotted purple butterfly
      red-bellied snake
       hognose snake
        hog sucker
        whalesucker
humpbacked whale
black-backed three-toed woodpecker
black horsefly
   redhorse
   red wolf
      wolf spider
       spider plant   silver maple
        snow plant   silver-haired bat
        snow flea   polka-dot batfish
      yellow fleabane   freshwater catfish
      yellow pondlily   waterscorpion
    stagnant pond snail   whip scorpion
         apple snail   whip-poor-will
       mayapple   desert willow
        mayfly   desert mariposa
        deerfly   white mariposa
     reindeer lichen   white turtlehead
      beard lichen   bog turtle
   foxglove beardtongue   northern bog lemming
red fox   northern cricket frog
red mangrove   mole cricket
dutchman's pipe   star-nosed mole
    indian pipe   starflower
    indian root   wildflower
striped coralroot   wild bleeding heart
striped maple   bleeding tooth
               cutleaf toothwort
          grapevine leafhopper
              froghopper
      barking treefrog

A Few Secrets

wild horses run
through the night.
I am awake,
comfortable in bed.
the exquisite light
of a plum-blue moon
bleeds magically.

a woman, old with age,
lent me secrets with
which to live.
the world is unknowable,
she said, yes unknowable,
except sometimes:
tasting wild plums
hot from the sun,
hearing a certain word
spoken as sunlight
slants, or touching
tips of fingers
on tips of fingers
you see, she said
everyone wants the same.
I come from a time
when horses were untamed
and women were
listened to and plums
were candy.
people inherit
power greed lust
now-a-days.
hold babies
take long walks
holding hands
give away
and laugh.
nectar is sweet
but plums can be dried
to be saved for later
for the harsh winter.

Emersion

Awakening, I sew myself
        a pair of pants and a shirt
from old blankets. Build a fire.
        Burn all remnants of my
tunnelings. Bury the entrance.
        I leave the forest as I found it.

In the distance of night, the city
        glistens, a hundred thousand
artificial fires; the sky domed with light.
        And I am drawn like a moth,
like a match, no sense to resist.

The highway twists like a neuron,
        with its axon of memory,
its axon of living. It was her:
        the passing touch while
I brushed my teeth at the double
        sink, the quick wink
during awkward dinner-guest
        conversation. It was her.

At morning, I trail the paper
        boy down the sidewalk,
making my way to the house
        where I once lived, where
I once slept-ate-loved-fought-left.
        The garage I built still
slightly tilted, the mail box still
        stuck like a question mark
in the front yard. Would she shun
        me? Embrace me?

She came out to rescue the morning
        paper from the yew.

Murmur

At the curb, you do not know
        me--ashen and sullen,
long-haired and bearded,
        more pauper than lover.

You take me in and I am in wonder:

blackberry tea,
        soothing like drips from a honeycomb.

hot-running water,
        seething like vapor off a river;

electric clippers,
        clattering like a murmuration of starlings;

television set,
        chattermagging like blue jays at a found nest;

            I am in wonder:
fingertips and palms,

psalms of lips

feaks of dark hair,

softness of stomach and labia.

            I am in wonder at us,
    sprawling,
  braided
in the sheets,
    such
      spectacular
      human
        wreckage.

Afterword

As a publisher, one searches for talented poets who matter and deserve a place in the light. Once every hundred books or so, one finds such a talent and then enjoys the unique collaboration that results. All too rarely, the poet achieves recognition and the publisher is privileged to make a worthy book; the reader benefits from both of their accomplishments.

Paul Brooke, however, offers the reader the duality of his talents as poet and photographer. And, in this duality, there exists the essential and wondrous tension of two forms of creative expression. Is it the photographer or the poet that touches us? The answer, I believe, is that it is both. The poems and the photographs have emerged from separate yet integrated places within the creative talent. The written images and the visual images complement, rebound, underscore, overlap, illuminate, but always add meaning and interpretation to the subject and to each other.

Finding a dual-creative talent is rare. Having two views of the creative moment is a treasure. Imagine, if you will, if we only had captured the thoughts and words of Ansel Adams at the moment he created his stark and detailed photographic images of Yosemite and the western mountains. When we see the famous *kyoka* wood-block prints of Katsushika Hokusai illustrating books of Japanese poetry, we are reminded of this rare and wondrous duality and integration of the creative viewpoint.

Paul Brooke is a trained biologist, a naturalist with native ties to Iowa. He has observed the land, the plants, the animals, the natural essence of this wonderful place called Iowa. His photographs are caught moments in time, images that can never be repeated, never seen by another again in the same way that he recorded them.

As a poet, Paul Brooke is a writer of images with native ties to Iowa. He has observed the people, the lives, the places, the loves and the losses, the natural rhythms of life in this special place called Iowa. His poems are of the heartland and of the heart land. They incise, spin and take on form and structure like the land and lives. He is a master of repetitive motifs, creating forms like rondos that re-curve and surprise the reader as the rolling hills of Iowa will momentarily dazzle and catch one unaware in places like the Loess Hills, or on the Balltown Road, or in the dream world of the Skunk River Valley.

Paul Brooke is a force of nature. He offers us choices. We can look for the light, or we can look for the matter. For the few fortunate enough to have the whole of Paul Brooke's creativity, we can choose light and matter. We can sit an evening and find fireflies and waxwings, hawthorns and raspberries, gain and loss, pain and love; perhaps even our own purpose and our own connection to this extraordinary place called Iowa that he has so masterfully imaged.

Publisher
Campbell & Lewis Publishers
February 2008